RICHARD BRAMWELL

Out of Place

Richard Bramwell

First published in 2018
by Richard Bramwell
www.richardbramwell.me.uk

ISBN 978-1-9998950-1-3

"Places, actual or imaginary, are fascinating. So are the spaces in-between."

Richard Bramwell first fell over in Yorkshire. He has since tripped abroad and stumbled from place to place across the British Isles. He now lives in north-west England with his wife, Eileen.

His first collection of poems, Signs of Life, was published in 2017.

To Eileen

Contents

Topography 1
Treasure 2
Dreams 4
Home Truth 6
Sleep Tight 7
The Art of Perception 8
A Risk of Intermittent Weather 9
Garden Centred 10
Airhead 11
Nursery Rumble 12
A Taste of History 14
The Mullets and Bars Forever 16
In the Night 20
Our Wall 22
Incontrovertible 24
When Summer Never Came 25
Nature Ramble 26
Natural Selection 28
Litterati 29
Wildfire 30
Only a Bird 32
Like a Leaf in Autumn 33
Outlandish 34
The Butterfly Effect 34
Topsy Turvy 35
Make Every Second Count 36
Awakening 37
Overture 38
Jumping to Conclusions 39

Nine Lives and Counting 39
A Perfect Couple 40
The Safe Place 42
Grown Old 44
A Rhyme at Bedtime 45
Displaced 46
A Breed Apart 48
Priceless 49
Knowing Your Place 50
The Hedge Cutter 54
Below Stairs 56
The Jade Palace 57
Bipolarity 58
Seasoning 59
I Know of a Young Man Whose Nose 60
Modern Life 60
Modern Art 61
Up-to-Date 61
Blackthorn Winter 62
Nature's Hope 63
Utterly Bemused 64
For Want of a Tittle 65
Fate 66

Notes 67

Topography

We look for patterns in the sky,
We trace designs upon the ground
And label where the features lie,
To navigate our way around.

A name identifies a place,
Describes it, brands it with a sign;
Imposes meaning on the space,
Complete with demarcation line.

Traditions weave throughout the land,
Conferring sentiment and worth;
Until events that are unplanned
Re-form the contours of the earth.

Unnatured patterns all decay,
Where sun has shone or winds have blown.
The tracks of man will lose their way
And nature will pursue its own.

Treasure

I've always loved my grandma's house,
It has a pleasant, homely feel.
Two-up, two-down, it isn't huge.
I used to go there after school.

I spent most time in her front room,
She'd read me stories and make tea,
And when I'd played and done enough,
I'd fall asleep on the settee.

Familiar, warm and welcoming,
The room became my home from home.
While grandma's hair turned silver white,
The front room always seemed the same:

Plants lined up on the window-sill,
Net curtains at the window panes;
Her comfy chair, her knitting bag,
A box for all her magazines.

And in one corner of the room
A cupboard, standing on the floor.
Like grandma's house, it was compact,
And had just one dark wooden door.

I asked her once, I said, "Grandma,
What is it that you keep in there?"
"That's where I keep my dreams," she said,
"To stop them flying through the air."

Well, this intrigued me even more.
My curiosity increased.
What treasures might I find in there?
I longed to have a look inside.

One afternoon, I saw my chance,
And crept past grandma while she dozed:
But though I tried and turned and pulled,
That little door stayed firmly closed.

Today, I live in grandma's house.
She left it in her will to me.
The cupboard now holds all my dreams,
Kept safely under lock and key.

Dreams

Each day I see you, growing up.

A few weeks old, you clutch my hand,
You gurgle and twitch and giggle with me.

At first, the days and nights stretch out,
So much for both of us to learn.
But then the weeks and months rush by,
And your first wriggles soon become
A shuffling crawl and tumbling steps,
And you can move — all by yourself.
And you can move — away from me.

On holiday, on Blackpool beach,
When you are eight and running free;
Your shorts are blue, the kite is red,
It's flying high above your head.

At school, you get on well enough;
Writing and sums, they're not for you.
You're sporting, active, on the move.
A touch-line mum, I watch you play.
You score the goal that wins a cup,
And bring your trophy home with pride.

You don't go on to college, no,
You go and get a useful job,
A plumber, like young Eddie Jones.
You learn the trade and earn good pay
And soon you'll set up on your own.

Today, it is your wedding day.
I cry, like every mother does.
I'm proud, of course, but worried too:
Will this mean I see less of you?

But then, if I live long enough,
Will you have children, two or three?
And will they come and visit me?
They'll keep me young and occupied,
And bring your childhood back to me.

My baby boy, my Oliver.
My heart aches when I think of you.

Nine months I carried you inside.
You lived two hours before you died.

Home Truth

Home is where the heart is.
East, west, home's best.
Be at home.

Make yourself at home.
Everything in its place.
A place like no other.

There's no place like home.
A no place is nowhere.
Home is where you make it.

Play at home or play away.
Travel broadens the mind.
Bad news travels fast.

Nothing to write home about.
Come home to roost.
Home, sweet home.

Sleep Tight

Amongst the rocks, just out of sight,
A little limpet held on tight.
He drank seawater every day
And never wandered off to play.

An octopus, all tentacles,
Mistook him for a barnacle:
It squirted ink and sucker-punched,
It wanted barnacle for lunch.

This 'barnacle' was clamped on fast:
The octopus gave up at last.
The little limpet gripped his rock —
He'd had a fright and was in shock.

He didn't see the seaweed wave,
He didn't hear the crabs applaud;
And while the sea breathed out and in
The little limpet laid his chin
Upon his rock-bed, in the bay,
And slept until another day.

The Art of Perception

Not at the bottom, looking up,
But at the top when looking down,
Her head would spin, she felt quite ill:
Amanda knew she needed help.

Her doctor diagnosed a cause,
But couldn't recommend a cure.
He told her it was vertigo
And should go of its own accord.

Amanda now was more distraught:
She had no fear of heights, as such,
Just dread of looking down the stairs.
Where could she turn to for support?

How could she manage on her own?
Go backwards? Crawl on hands and knees?
Or close her eyes when at the top,
From where the only way is down?

The cure came to her unawares,
Whilst browsing through a bookshop's shelves:
She opened up a picture-book
And found the answer to her prayers.

A book whose drawings give her pleasure
Has cured her of her phobia:
The way she looks at stairs has changed,
All thanks to artist M. C. Escher.

A Risk of Intermittent Weather

The day is misbehaving,
the forecast was for rain,
and yet the sun is shining,
it really is a pain.

The forecasters examine
their data and their maps,
and from these they determine
what we will get . . . perhaps.

They use the best computers,
I'm sure they're all good guys,
I only have one question —
why don't they use their eyes?

The view outside their windows
must be the same as mine,
so why forecast tornadoes
when here, the weather's fine?

"Storms forecast, and more beside,
approaching from the east!"
How come then, when I'm outside,
the wind is from the west?

I don't care what they forecast
when I'm asleep, at night;
but when I'm having breakfast
I want the forecast right!

Garden Centred

Old gardeners read the clouds and leaves,
'Oak before ash' and other notions;
Today there are much better guides —
The garden centre's main promotions.

When aisles are packed with Christmas cards,
Poinsettias, ornaments and trees
It's Autumn, and it's time to buy
Spring bulbs and flashing LEDs.

Sweet Valentines and Easter eggs
Proclaim to us that Winter's here:
Dwarf daffodils and hyacinths —
And calendars 'Reduced to clear'.

Spring is the gardener's busy time,
Announced by colourful displays
With rows of Summer bedding plants
In tubs and troughs and six-pack trays.

Umbrellas, boots and 'Back to School'
Are signs that Summer's on the way:
The water-butts have all sold out
But barbecues 'Half-Price Today'.

Airhead

He took the selfies as a dare
to make some photos he could share;
they'd be superb, his plan was ace,
because he knew the perfect place.

Courageously he climbed so high
he felt that he could touch the sky.
He smiled and waved, like heroes did;
he'd be a star, not just a kid.

His final pose was air guitar —
he felt as though he walked on air —
played one long riff, the chords were grand
and, full of sound, he hit the ground.

Our little Jimmy wasn't harmed:
the tallest building in the land
had been his father's garden shed.
He clutched his phone, and went to bed.

Nursery Rumble

Old Mother Hubbard
Looked in a cupboard,
Wanting some curds and whey,
When down came a spider to sit down beside her —
Ma Hubbard just brushed it away.
Three blind mice squealed
When they heard what she did;
Another mouse ran up the clock and hid.

The clock struck one and she put her coat on,
She decided to go for a walk:
And after some exercise and fresh air,
She'd call on a neighbour for tea and a talk.
Ma Hubbard set off to see her friend, Jill,
But she took the wrong road, heading downhill:
The way became steep and a little scary
And then, quite contrary, she met Mary.

Mary had ten little lambs,
Their fleece was white as mud:
But Mary's farm, the fields, the flowers,
Were just a front, a dud:
For hey diddle diddle, she'd gone on the fiddle,
And was claiming back tax on her flock;
She had to watch out, 'cos if she got caught,
She'd land in the hickory dickory dock.

When Mary let on to what she had done,
Ma Hubbard was quiet, then said with a smile,
"I have an idea, let's both have some fun:
You need to lie low, disappear for a while.
You'll need a disguise, so no-one will guess,
We'll change your hair and change your dress
And use a new name — try Little Bo Peep.
There's much more to life than just counting
    sheep!"

So that was how Mary 'lost' her sheep,
And soon became — very rich — Bo Peep:
All the King's horses and all the King's men
Wouldn't find shepherdess Mary again.
And Old Mother Hubbard? She hadn't a care,
A regular cheque from abroad saw to that:
Her cupboards were full, no longer left bare:
And her little doggie had now grown quite fat.

A Taste of History

In central America, long ago,
there sprouted a tree that gave us cocoa.
The Mayans and Aztecs used it at first,
in a potent brew to sate their lords' thirst.

Marauding Spaniards set eyes on the pods —
which locals revered as gifts of the gods —
they carried their bounty back home to Spain
where 'choc-o-la-te-' was met with acclaim.

The costly beans were consumed with a passion
as drinking chocolate became quite a fashion.
Chocolate for years was enjoyed as a drink
until creative minds began to think:

how could they make it solid, fit to eat,
and so might produce an edible treat.
Two Swiss men, surrounded by alps to climb,
were looking for new ways to pass the time:

they'd done all they could with their cuckoo clocks
and tried adding milk to the chocolate blocks.
Sweet milk chocolate was what people desired:
the makers grew rich, and could have retired.

But for the inventors, it wasn't right,
they wanted their chocolate not brown, but WHITE —
as pure as the mountains and alpine air
that tasted of chocolate but looked more fair.

They laid out the beans to bleach in the sun,
but this didn't work, the beans remained dun.
Tincture of polar bear, essence of snow,
for the white answer they searched high and low.

Their break-through came in 1936:
with Milkybar they found the perfect mix.
The gnomes of Nestlé earned the nation's thanks
and, better still, they soon made lots of francs!

What had been dark or brown was now made white
and chocoholics feasted with delight.
As white chocolate sold in land after land,
competitors challenged the Nestlé brand.

'Let's send for the Three Marketeers,' they cried,
'to boost the sales of Milkybars world-wide.'
The ad-men proposed that, to tempt the masses,
they should use a pale young cowboy with glasses.

Quite why he appealed is a mystery
but the rest, as they say, is history!

The Mullets and Bars Forever

My tale is of a Washing line,
Not made of plastic, string or twine:
A line that starts from land in Sweden,
Through England, to the west's new Eden;
A line that crosses land and sea,
Thousands of miles from A to B.

In distant Ages, now called Dark,
(And using longboats, not an ark),
The Vikings travelled to our coast
And, while some pirates pillaged, most
Began to like it here and tarried;
They settled down and even married.

One settlement on land they claimed
Belonged to Wassa, and was named
After the man: Wassa-ing-tun —
A place we now call Washington.
The name thus used for farm and town,
The people also handed down.

In time, as hamlets grew, and towns,
Although there were some ups and downs
Like Normans, plagues and other things
Disturbing to the rule of kings,
The tribes of England became one
And thought themselves second to none.

The English looked beyond their shore;
For all their land, they wanted more.
They went in ships, explored and traded;
Some went as soldiers and invaded.
That noble pirate, Francis Drake,
Grabbed all the booty he could take.

The British Empire grew gigantic,
And spread across the north Atlantic.
In faith, or greed, or desperation,
Shiploads embarked on emigration.
The ground they claimed was tilled and weeded,
And soon provided all they needed.

Britain received their surplus goods,
Exotic fruits, and furs, and woods.
Tobacco came by way of trade —
Imagine what a sight this made:
Their lordships in their fancy ruffs,
Filling their pipes and taking puffs.

John Washington, then young and pale,
Was one of many who set sail.
He was descended from the line
Of Viking settlers near the Tyne.
He left his family a note,
'I'm going west, aboard a boat.'

He settled down, he made his stand,
He married, and soon owned some land.
The sons of John then fathered more,
And by hard work they set great store;
They laboured long, cleared scrub and marsh,
Conditions for them all were harsh.

It also hurt them, every day,
To see their riches float away.
By law, all trading was protected,
And hefty taxes were collected.
The profits from the new-found lands
All found their way to British hands.

It rankled, it stuck in the throat,
To pay a tax but have no vote.
The colonists then left their farms
And went to fight, to take up arms.
They had a feisty disposition,
And fought against this imposition.

The British tried to restore order,
Confine these upstarts to their border.
This military subjugation
Helped forge from colonies a nation.
It cost too much to wage a war
Upon a distant, hostile shore.

When freedom from the Crown was won
George Washington, John's great-grandson,
Became the nation's president,
The capital's first resident.
In recognition of his fame,
They gave the capital his name.

Another fact is quite surprising
About the colonists' uprising:
They chose the arms of Washington
To base their nation's flag upon.
The shapes that look like stars and stripes
Are not stars in the sky, nor pipes:

These emblems, brought across the sea,
Have special names in heraldry.
The three red stars, set in a row,
Are spurs, called mullets long ago;
The stripes are bars — one belt, one fess —
Both symbols of a knight's prowess.

And thus, the line of Washington,
From place to person and so on,
Spanned land and sea, and passed on genes;
And thanks to George it also means
The U.S. flag, of stripes and stars,
Is really mullets with some bars.

In the Night

Downstairs, enjoying time alone,
Emma browses on her phone;
upstairs, her daughter, fast a—

"Mummy, mummy! I can't sleep!"
The plaintive wail curls down the stairs
and penetrates her mother's ears.

Emma hurries to her daughter,
"What's wrong, sweetie, what's the matter?"

"Mummy," sobs a tearful Katie,
"a spider, it's come to eat me!
It's big and hairy, over there!"

Her mother looks round everywhere,
but there's no spider to be seen:
"I think you must have had a dream,
there's nothing here, I've looked all round;
the window's closed, you're safe and sound."

"I'm leaving on your bedside light,
nothing will hurt you here tonight,
so don't upset yourself like this."

She gives her daughter one last kiss,
doing her best to calm her fears,
and makes her way back down the stairs.

"Mummy, mummy, I can't sleep!"
Twice more the cry from Katie comes
and each time, Emma does the same:
she rushes up the stairs once more,
maternal instinct to the fore.

Katie sobs, she's seen a spider,
it's got huge fangs, it's there beside her.

Emma reassures her daughter,
reminds her of what she's taught her,
how to relax and go to sleep,
"And I don't want another peep!"

Downstairs, she thinks, 'I can't go on,
that's three times now, it isn't fun.
I'm fussing too much, this is wrong:
I will ignore her, and be strong.
She's 8 years old, she's old enough,
for her own good I must be tough.'

"Mummy, I'm scared! The spider's here!
It's hurting! It's got hold of me!"
The high-pitched cry is now a scream —
but Emma knows she must be firm,
and concentrates on what she's reading.

At last, she thinks she is succeeding:
there is no further sound from Katie.

Before she turns in for the night
she looks into her daughter's room
where all is quiet, all seems calm —
but of her daughter there's no sign!
A cold sweat runs down Emma's spine.
Her daughter's gone, what can it mean?

One thing disturbs the peaceful scene:
the bed, the place where Katie lies,
is covered with a web of cries.

Our Wall

It was on the Monday morning
    the brickie came to call:
We wanted him to do a job,
    to build a new back wall.
"You've got a problem here," he said,
    "the height is far too tall.
If I balanced on a ladder,
    one slip and I could fall."

It was on the Tuesday morning
    the scaffolder came round:
"You've got a problem here," he said,
    and showed us what he'd found.
"See how the paving slopes away —
    you've got a sort of mound.
I can't set up my scaffold there —
    it must have level ground."

It was on the Wednesday morning
    the flagging man came out:
We showed him the uneven bits
    we wanted straightening out.
He gave his pick a mighty swing
    and then he gave a shout —
He'd broken through a water pipe —
    we'd water gushing out.

It was on the Thursday morning
    the water board came by:
We asked if they could mend the leak,
    they said that they would try.
They moved the flags and dug a hole
    and piled the rubble high
But soon they did the job and made
    the flags all straight and dry.

It was on the Friday morning
    the scaffolder came back:
He brought his poles and nuts and bolts,
    to put us back on track;
But as he swung the final pole
    there was a mighty crack —
Our window looks a picture now —
    it's covered with a sack.

The next day was a Saturday,
    no workmen came to call:
We peered around the sack and saw
    a sight that made us cry —
Some lout had come round in the night
    and painted our old wall!
There was a sort of signature,
    'B' ... something ... something ... 'Y'.
We've done our best to scrub it off —
    you know the reason why:
Because on the Monday morning
    the brickie's due to call ...

Incontrovertible

A thing I never can believe
Is why some wise and solemn folk
Spread stories that the Earth is round:
Such falsehoods are beyond a joke.

The Sun comes up, rides high, and sets,
A daily pattern all may mark:
Across the lofty firmament
Its pathway clearly is an arc.

And here below, upon the Earth,
Our feet are firmly on the ground:
We'd fall off or hang upside down
If as they claim, the Earth were round.

To say this level world's a globe
Is patently a foolish notion.
A simple question will suffice:
How can a sphere possess an ocean?

A round Earth is nonsensical:
Tip up a bowl and it is clear
No lake or ocean could remain
In an inverted hemisphere.

Brave mariners use charts to plot
Their course upon the seven seas:
They don't set sail with magic globes,
And unicorns don't grow on trees.

The Earth is flat,
And that is that.

When Summer Never Came

In the year of Our Lord, and mad King George,
Called one thousand eight hundred and sixteen,
Countless thousands died and harvests were lean
Because of one fiery, underground forge.

A foul cloud of ash cloaked the atmosphere:
A massive volcano had blown its top —
Causing the cycle of seasons to stop.
Poor weather persisted throughout the year.

Across the known world, the temperature fell,
The sun obscured by an overcast sky;
Their crops, their livestock and people would die,
For many, their world became a cold hell.

Bitter, cold weather benighted the ground
For months, not just odd days of cruel frost;
Seeds couldn't be planted, harvests were lost,
Prices rose for what poor food could be found.

Snow fell in June and people went sleighing.
Food supplies dwindled, passions grew inflamed;
The rich or the heavens, who could be blamed?
Some joined in riots, others in praying.

Blighted and starving, no lives stayed the same,
Then came a new scourge: disease spread its hand,
Bringing more pain and death to the cold land,
In the year when summer never came.

Nature Ramble

I wandered out amongst the hills
But never saw the daffodils:
The cloud came down, all wet and grey,
And I completely lost my way.

Although I soon had quite a thirst
I wasn't worried, not at first:
My mobile phone would see me right,
With GPS instead of sight.

But would a signal reach me here?
A quick search soon confirmed my fear:
I couldn't blame some awkward crag —
My phone was in my other bag!

Dejected, feeling such a fool,
I trod into a muddy pool:
With sodden steps, I lumbered on,
All pleasure in the walk now gone.

The view was blanked out, all around
And I could barely see the ground:
I took more care of where I trod
And then I saw it, something odd —

A sight to raise my spirits up —
A celandine or buttercup:
I bent down for a closer look,
It wasn't in my nature book.

The small sweet-wrapper that I saw
Meant someone passed this way before:
Perhaps I was still on the track,
And had a chance of getting back.

Out of the gloom, a shape emerged —
A person! How my spirit surged:
Two souls, both lost, but now together,
Engaged with nature (and the weather).

Natural Selection

See forests in an acorn
And a mountain in a rock;
See oceans in a droplet
And a homeland in the dust.

Rip timber from a forest,
Gouge metals from a mountain;
Dump sewage in the oceans
And build borders on the land.

Litterati

Food wrappers, cartons, paper cups,
A toy car's wheel, a broken pen,
Squashed cans, crushed plastic, bits of glass,
A shoe that will not fit again:

Abandoned bits of people's lives,
They lie there fallen, lost or thrown,
By accident or conscious act
Discarded, provenance unknown.

If they were in some special place
A future archaeologist
Might come and excavate the site,
Conduct a survey, make a list.

Excitement comes on windy days:
The lighter pieces lift and spin
But heavy items will not stir,
Unmoved by air's indiscipline.

Unlike the litter people drop,
Leaves decompose and blow away
But plastic stuff and metal things
They won't decay, they're there to stay,

Untidiness embossed in dirt.
Detritus of a careless kind.
Poor tribute to our Mother Earth,
Memorials of humankind.

Wildfire

He held in his left hand a cigarette end
And opened the window, approaching the bend;
The stub he tossed out disappeared in the grass,
Alongside the plastic, food wrappers and glass.

On a verge that was parched, from weeks without rain,
The heat from that one butt ignited a flame
That flickered a moment, then flared and lengthened:
Its first feeble glimmer blossomed and strengthened.

In moments, the whole of the verge was alight,
Hot tongues of fire dancing, the grass burning bright.
Whipped on by a keen wind, sparks swirled up and flew
And a blazing inferno rapidly grew.

Prime acres of woodland, beyond the low fence,
Against such an onslaught had little defence.
Leaves shrivelled and withered in fierce, intense heat,
Small creatures and insects succumbed in defeat.

In the woodland, a lodge, used for holidays,
Was completely consumed by the raging blaze.
No guests had been there on the day of the fire,
As the weekend retreat turned into a pyre.

Exhausted at length, the hot flames subsided,
Starved of the fuel the forest provided.
When the dense, acrid smoke was cleared by the breeze,
It unveiled the stark, blackened remnants of trees,

With a lifeless blanket of ash on the ground
And unnatural stillness, an absence of sound.
From one careless act that sparked the ignition,
The woodland was changed, beyond recognition.

The lodge was a write-off; including the sign
That contained in its rules and advice this line,
'If the weather turns cold, then we recommend:
Use our wood-burning stove. Enjoy your weekend.'

Only a Bird

A brown-coloured, ground-nesting bird,
Whose numbers have dropped by a third;
    It's on the red list,
    But would it be missed
If species extinction occurred?

Its diet of insects and seeds
Helped keep down the pests and the weeds,
    But farmers saw cost
    Of spring shoots they lost
And blamed it on how the lark feeds.

To land on an epicure's plate
For thousands of birds was their fate;
    With British taste sated,
    For those that migrated
The hunters abroad lay in wait.

But when it has died or been slain
Some traces would surely remain:
    Some music or verse —
    Could this reimburse
Not hearing the skylark again?

Would many be likely to mourn
The loss of this herald of dawn?
    Some speck in the sky,
    Mere mote in the eye,
Why feel, in the slightest, forlorn?

Do humans have no space to share
With birds now increasingly rare?
    If our acts give rise
    To one bird's demise,
Is it in our nature to care?

Like a Leaf in Autumn

Ash trees grow stunted with disease,
Malignant spores defile the air:
Malaise is blowing in the breeze.

Cut-price contagion crossed the seas,
Imported seedlings of despair;
Ash trees grow stunted with disease.

Our woods are full of absentees,
No longer ashen-faced and fair:
Malaise is blowing in the breeze.

Beneath the earth, pale filigrees
Conspire to strip the branches bare;
Ash trees grow stunted with disease.

In hedgerows and in limestone leas
The common ash is all too rare.
Malaise is blowing in the breeze.

Loose-leaf and leafless by degrees,
Their keys a barren fruit will bear.
Ash trees grow stunted with disease:
Malaise is blowing in the breeze.

Outlandish

I saw a strange creature go by
With five legs and only one eye;
It saw me and winked —
Or maybe it blinked —
Perhaps it's not forward, just shy.

The Butterfly Effect

There once was a chrysalis blue
Inside which a butterfly grew.
And on the same day
It fluttered away,
High winds blew a tree down in Crewe.

Topsy Turvy

The Earth is round.
In our daily life, we know
From the things we experience
The reality of the situation.
We know
We do not tumble from the ground.
We do not live life upside down.
Do they not know the gravity of their position?
It is a foolish superstition.
Such a claim is incredible.
In this day and age
We know
The Earth is flat.

(*now read from bottom to top*)

Make Every Second Count

Second sight, second wind, a second crop,
each one of these things is desirable;
for nuclear reactors and parachutes
a fail-safe back-up is advisable.

First-timers don't always come off the best:
who discovered that plant was poisonous?
Without someone else, duets will fall flat,
conversations would be monotonous.

Two heads are better at finding a way,
ask a friend or partner, husband or wife;
and in medical matters, there's no doubt,
a second opinion may save your life.

Let others contend to be number one,
for I am content as second — to none.

Awakening

Dispel the shadows that descend at night,
Discover lifelines kindled with the dawn;
Embrace the paths and patterns of the light.

Dislodge disturbing dreams, all trace of fright,
Emerge from fantasies, untimely torn;
Dispel the shadows that descend at night.

Awaken nerves to sense and eyes to sight,
Disown the careless shades that sleep has worn;
Embrace the paths and patterns of the light.

Dissolve the bonds that hold your body tight,
Salute each day with a dishevelled yawn;
Dispel the shadows that descend at night.

Resolve to journey where day's beams invite,
Discern how shifting shadows are redrawn;
Embrace the paths and patterns of the light.

Distil the way from features now made bright,
Pursue ideas conceived and actions born.
Dispel the shadows that descend at night;
Embrace the paths and patterns of the light.

Overture

He'd played the piece so many times before,
practised, rehearsed, performed, in this same hall;
he knew how it should feel, he knew the score.

Backstage, he followed through the same routine;
with care, he took his violin from its case,
tightened the bow, made sure that all was clean.

He was on edge, and yet he felt composed;
his hands and his whole body felt prepared.
Seated in his place, mind and senses poised:

the instruments are tuned to concert pitch,
a hush descends, the maestro's baton raised —
the same notes sound again — and yet, and yet . . .

Jumping to Conclusions

When Susan declared she had 'nits'
I'd visions of larvae and zits.
"Oh, no, Uncle Matt,"
She laughed, "it's not that!
They're chunky wool cardigan kits."

Nine Lives and Counting

We bought our pet cat a soft bed
To rest and to lay down his head,
So where does he choose
To go for a snooze?
He sleeps on the doormat instead.

A Perfect Couple

Every other Tuesday,
They caught the bus to town;
Maureen went and Edwin went
To their usual stamping ground.

They went as dancing partners,
To the tea dance in the hall.
She was nimble, not too plump;
He was sprightly, not too tall.

Each time, they'd leave their hat and coat,
And head for the same place.
They knew the other regulars,
Each smiling, friendly face.

They'd do a quick-step and the waltz,
Crossing the floor in harmony,
Sit at their table, chat with friends,
Dunk a digestive in their tea.

They didn't live in the same house:
He lived nearby, in the next street,
And in their normal, daily lives
Their paths would hardly ever meet.

By day, she knitted granny squares,
The needles clicking slickly;
Her fingers moved with practised ease,
And each new piece grew quickly.

By day, he potted seedlings on,
His fingers moving gently;
Thinking of what might blossom
If nurtured patiently.

Every other Tuesday,
They caught the bus to town;
Edwin in the odd weeks,
And Maureen in the even.

The Safe Place

I put it there, I know I did,
But no, it isn't there,
And soon I'm hunting high and low,
In panic and despair.

I put it carefully away
And then my life moved on . . .
Until the day I want the thing —
And find that it has gone.

The place was safe and sensible,
An easy place to find —
Except — its exact whereabouts
Have somehow slipped my mind.

I rummage through each cupboard shelf,
I root in every drawer;
Slow down, I tell myself, breathe deep,
You've looked in there before.

I can't afford to waste more time,
And give up on my quest;
I must make do with something else,
Although it's second best.

I get on with my life again;
The days pass, one by one;
Then suddenly, by accident,
I chance to come upon —

The thing that so frustrated me —
That made me doubt myself —
It wasn't lost or thrown away,
Just sitting on a shelf.

The thing I put in its safe place
Has been there all along:
I gently close the cupboard door
And hum a little song.

Grown Old

I'm no fun to be with, I'm told:
At parties, I'm left in the cold;
My head's full of stories,
But all of past glories —
I'm yesterday's model: I'm old.

If I try to drink and be bold
There's one part that won't be controlled:
I soon become madder
Because of my bladder —
There's only so much it will hold!

My hips and my teeth aren't my own,
The hair on my head's thinly sown;
I'm not made to last,
My sell-by date's passed,
Forgetful and accident-prone.

And yes, I do like a good moan . . .
Dance music today makes me groan:
Just digital noise
With no style or poise
Oh, bring back the old gramophone.

Then one day when I go to town
The shopkeepers all wear a frown:
The power's been cut
And some shops have shut
Because their computers are down.

I show them what I learned at school
Without an electronic tool:
I add in my head —
"That's awesome", they said.
I'm yesterday's model: I'm cool.

A Rhyme at Bedtime

I remember things that rhyme,
Ideas that chime in my head:
Words like sounds that swirl around
As I fall asleep in bed.

I shut my eyes and somewhere deep
My mind breaks out in dreams:
I drift and spin and come to rest
Where nothing is as it seems.

All befuddled, mixed and muddled,
In a hurry, scurrylous:
Running late, so nearly there,
Hit the spot and miss the bus.

Ten tall tent pegs on a wall,
Swimming without getting wet:
Shadows melt and turn to flowers
Flying in a jumbo jet.

Something rumbles, someone mumbles,
Sun tries to break through the curtain:
I know I'm lying in my bed,
I'm safe — but am I certain?

Displaced

The sudden clatter startled him —
A sudden hammering of sound
A terrifying gush of noise
That shattered everything around.

His senses snoozing, quite relaxed,
He had been sitting in his chair
A novel open on his lap
His mind had wandered off elsewhere.

For moments he felt terrified
His vision blurred, his breath on hold —
His heartbeat raced, his stomach churned;
Head swimming, sick and clammy cold

With nervous glance he looked around —
The walls, the ceiling and the floor
All seemed intact, no damage done;
Nothing was coming through the door.

His eyes belied the noise he heard:
Inside the room was still and calm
Nothing was shaking or disturbed
No monster come to do him harm.

He could not feel, he could not see
Beyond the curtained window-pane,
But now he placed the noise he heard:
The tuneless din of heavy rain.

The mad tap-dance continued on
But now his racing pulse grew slack
He felt less muzzy and confused
His spongy brain was coming back.

His equilibrium returned,
Untensed his limbs, relaxed his face
And then, annoyed, he realised
His book had closed — he'd lost his place.

A Breed Apart

Sir Gerald owned a large estate;
good fortune and inheritance
provided for his daily needs.
He loved to play as much as work:
St Grouse's Day would see him gone
to join a party on the moors.
Dressed in his barbour and his tweeds
he'd shoot a line and have a blast.
Most of the bag would be sold on,
but he'd bring home a brace or two.

Tom was a gardener for Sir Gerald,
to whom he'd always touch his cap.
He came from local country stock
and had a tied house in the grounds.
He took great pride in his domain,
tending heirlooms in the loam.
Tom worked long hours in the fresh air
in waterproofs or in shirt-sleeves,
weeding, feeding, chopping off heads,
mulching, grafting and potting on.

Tom and Sir Gerald each had a boy,
who was for both their pride and joy.
Growing up close by, far from a town,
they played together in holiday time.
If dressed alike, they could be brothers,
until they opened their mouths to speak:
then you could tell one from the other —
not by their accent but the glint —
not silver spoon or piece of straw,
but metal braces in the jaw.

Priceless

The stranger heard them talking in the bar,
He sipped his drink and strained to hear some more,
Something about a casket full of gems;
They chatted on and didn't notice him.

He drank up when they did and followed them;
The tall one was John, the one with the gems.
He shadowed John home, found out his address,
And for a few days kept watch on the place.

He made sure that no-one was in the house
And made his entry, quiet as a mouse.
He wasted no time, a quick in and out,
Just took what he came for and that was it.

When John reached in for the casket next day
His treasure had gone, the cupboard was bare:
All he'd collected throughout his career
The gems he'd honed and polished, year by year.

He had no time to wallow in his plight,
The curtain call was 8 o'clock tonight.
With luck, the audience wouldn't notice it
If he looked a fool and ad-libbed a bit.

They'd paid to see him; he'd money to earn;
He'd go on and give them a funny turn.

In times gone by, when wolves could fly,
enormous dragons ruled the sky.
Dwellers on land, who had no wings,
such beasts were puny, lesser things.
Those timid wretches could be found
scraping a living on the ground.
In one place was a deep ravine
where, at one end, there could be seen
a giant — not of flesh and bone —
it was a monstrous cliff of stone.

The creatures on the valley floor
gazed at the scar with fear and awe.
The limestone crag, that loomed so tall,
was guardian rock and prison wall.
It blocked the way, it blocked the light,
so half the day was dark as night.
And yet, for mortals at its base
this tower held the sky in place,
protected them and kept them safe,
so they believed, such was their faith.

According to an ancient scribe
one human from the valley tribe,
unheeding of his fate of birth,
aspired to rise above the earth,
do what no man had done before,
and venture from the valley floor.
Unlike the others of his clan
he grew to be a fearless man:
his name was Hræfn, son of Æsc;
he was adventurous — and rash.

Intelligent and quick to learn,
he'd endless energy to burn,
for when each hard day's work was done
he wouldn't rest, he wanted fun:
he'd break off twigs to play a game,
showed others how to do the same.
Sometimes the games they played turned rough,
but Hræfn joined in, he was tough;
even when hurt, he'd never weep.
His limbs were strong, his voice grew deep.

With night-black hair and bearded jaw
he was a little boy no more.
His blue-grey eyes of younger days
now showed a dark brown, piercing gaze.
Courageously, he'd often do
some tasks that others thought taboo:
he'd call down wolves to take the dead —
they did no harm once they were fed.
He took the lead, and showed no fear,
as though his path through life were clear.

As well as hours of fruitless toil
to coax some goodness from the soil,
the humans foraged when they could,
around their barren neighbourhood.
Young Hræfn might go off alone,
attracted by a rock or stone,
but what enticed him even more
were those occasions when he saw
above the valley, way up high,
a pod of dragons flying by.

He wondered where they went at night,
what path they took when out of sight.
He hopped and ran and with one bound
jumped high above the rocky ground,
but every time, he tumbled back,
condemned to tread his low-born track.
He dreamed of somehow breaking free,
so that he'd find a way to see
that fabled place concealed from men —
the land where dragons had their den.

He wasn't paired up with a mate
and so, before it was too late,
resolved to bring to life his dream,
and activate his daring scheme.
He picked a smooth and shiny stone
to serve him as a talisman.
And then appeared a wondrous sign:
he saw a triple-rainbow shine.
Encouraged by this awesome sight
he had but little sleep that night.

Before all shadows cleared the land
he started out, as he had planned:
dressed in his rags, with staff and bag,
he headed for the fearsome crag.
Familiar trails all faded out
but Hræfn never felt in doubt;
the landmark was too huge to miss
and soon he reached the edifice,
both feared and worshipped by all men,
where he might find the dragons' den.

The summit was still wreathed in mist
as up he climbed, hand over fist.
At last, he reached the highest ledge,
and slowly scrambled to its edge.
And there he saw it, broad and high —
the gateway to the land of sky.
He stepped into the dragon's lair —
its floor was nothing more than air.
He dreamed of soaring far and wide
as he began his earth-born glide.

The stone-sprite fell from Hræfn's hand,
and scuttled back to its own land.
The limestone crag, seen from afar,
these days is known as Raven Scar.

The Hedge Cutter

Weeping Tom, we call it,
The painting on the wall;
It hangs above the staircase,
Well over six feet tall.

One morning, twenty years ago,
Old Tom was working at his trade,
Thinning out the lower growth
Of a hedgerow he had laid;

By the edge of Bottom Pasture,
Clad in leather gloves and coat,
Bending, careful at his work,
Culling each unwanted shoot.

Also that day the master's son
Had saddled up his pony,
And though he was just ten years old,
Young James went for his ride alone.

He rode along the causeway,
Proceeding at a gentle pace,
Taking in the morning air,
The warmth of sunlight on his face.

Suddenly his pony swerved,
Startled by a bird that flapped
Out of the grass beside the trail:
The pony bolted, James was trapped,

Careering headlong down Bank Field.
He lost the reins, just held on tight,
But as the bottom hedge loomed close
The boy's excitement turned to fright.

Hearing the crash, Tom turned at once
And pushed through the thicket to James:
The pony, struggling to get free,
Was dragging his rider with him:

Tom knew he had to save the boy
Whose foot was held fast in the stirrup;
He gripped his billhook, swung his arm,
And sliced clean through the leather strap.

Tom calmed the pony, lifted James,
And led them back towards the hall.
A servant met them in the yard
And Tom explained about the fall.

With care they carried James indoors,
The boy was badly shaken;
But thankfully although he'd been
Scratched and bruised he'd no bones broken.

Tom felt a dampness on his cheek,
And with his kerchief brushed it dry.
It wasn't sweat but blood he saw:
A thorn had pierced him in the eye.

Weeping Tom, we call it,
The painting on the wall;
It hangs above the staircase,
A tribute from us all.

Below Stairs

'Be in the world but not of it.'
The life he led was set apart,
Reminded daily of his calling
To live an upright, simple life.

Do not put on grand, fancy airs,
Forsake indulgence above stairs.
Avoid temptation, do no sin;
Receive no comfort from a wife.

Remain untainted, clean and pure,
Rise above man's baser nature.
All this he thought as he lay still
And floorboards creaked above his head.

One day, when briefly let outside,
A lady begged him to confide,
"Pray tell me your station", she asked.
"A priest hole, my lady", he said.

"Kept below stairs for the sake of a king,
I pray in the dark and silently sing."

The Jade Palace

Along the ancient road, at dawn,
no sound disturbs the limpid air;
even the colours here are muted,
soft ochres and a gentle fawn.

Before the sun soars in the sky,
and makes outside too hot to bear,
I turn onto a dusty track
to where the time-worn ruins lie.

I enter through a broken wall,
and pass into the rooms beyond.
Stillness now reigns within this place;
there's not another living soul.

I stand, imagining the scene,
retainers hurrying to serve
the guests who call upon the court —
and then there would have been the green:

these walls that now rise dull and bare
would once have glowed with precious jade,
fine carvings and choice furnishings —
a gleaming sight beyond compare.

The fingers of a jewelled hand
caress a costly ornament,
tracing the contours of the shape —

I'm broken from my reverie:
'Who for phone order twenty-three?'

Bipolarity

(read from top to bottom and/or from bottom to top)

White is black.
Grey is a shade of black.
Grey is a shade of white.

White is a colour.
Black is the absence of colour.
Grey is a colour.

Colour is perception upon reflection.
White is a pigment of our imagination.
Black is the combination of all colours.

Black contains white.
White goods are for sale on the black market.
A black-and-white photograph is made from
    shades of grey.

A zebra is black and white.
Things can be black and white at the same time.
Think of a chessboard, a barcode, yin and yang.

Ash is white.
Burning coal gives ash.
Coal is black.

Black is a shade of grey.
White is a shade of grey.
Black is white.

Seasoning

俳
句

snowdrops
scatterings of light
ground-breaking

○

spines unfurl
bright air touches skin
feet emerge

○

summer rain
fragrance of wet earth
droplets glisten

○

a puddle
trodden underfoot
holds the sky

○

broken kite
half-buried in sand
sky high dream

○

crinkled leaves
patterns of sunlight
loam litter

I Know of a Young Man Whose Nose

I know of a young man whose nose
Casts shadows wherever he goes:
When he walks about
You soon hear him shout,
"I've trod on my nose with my toes!"

Modern Life

In my day, the birds used to twitter,
And spam tasted good in a fritter.
Now twitters and spam
Aren't bird-songs or ham,
But some kind of virtual litter.

Modern Art

What counts as a great work of art?
What's special, what sets it apart?
It's not style or form,
Not newness or norm,
But with how much cash we will part.

Up-to-Date

In these days, when two people meet,
Their contact is very discreet:
All physical passion
Is quite out of fashion,
Replaced with a text or a tweet.

Blackthorn Winter

Our home is blacked out by the snow
as heavy falls bring power lines down.
The lane is blocked, that leads to town.
We are cut off, no way to go.

Blizzards of swirling, crystal flakes
descend relentlessly to earth,
blundering to their silent death.
Beneath their weight, a tree branch breaks.

The landscape that we know is drowned,
cocooned beneath an icy shroud;
familiar features blotted out,
transformed into amorphous mounds.

Under a baleful, leaden sky
a gloomy pallor grips the place,
all colour bleached in cold embrace,
and one black crow flies slowly by.

Nature's Hope

The sun now doesn't climb as high
Blue sky takes on a paler hue
Chill dampness haunts the morning air
All signs that winter will be due.

Green leaves grow withered, turn and fall
Marks of decay are all around
Few blossoms raise their fragile heads
But new life slumbers underground.

Utterly Bemused

Some words sound phoney when written for money.
Some rhymes take the biscuit, others don't suit,
loading a line with more than it can bear,
so the sounds that we hear wear down the ear.

Some verses won't scan, do what we can,
their metre's upended for want of a foot;
the images conveyed are pale and wan,
and whether revisions improve them is moot.

The letters of some lines are lifeless and bare,
honed to the bone, all interest gone;
a tour through the stanzas elucidates how
the rhythms turn sour when arrayed in a row.

No matter how carefully words are laid,
they fail to impress when they're read and said.
I'm sorry, I'm through, I've just had enough:
My rhymes remain rough as I pocket the dough.

For Want of a Tittle

For want of a tittle, the i was too little.
For lack of a vowel, the word was inconsonant.

For want of a consonant, the noun was improper.
For lack of a subject, the phrase lost its point.

For want of a dagger, the footnote was lost.
For lack of a footnote, the meaning was lost.

For want of allusion, the nouns were abstracted.
For lack of a context, the text was protracted.

For want of a pronoun, the line lost its threading.
For lack of conjunction, the words lost their heading.

For want of connection, the clause was omitted.
For lack of ellipsis, the loss went unnoticed.

For want of a comma, the passage changed sense.
For lack of a timeframe, the verb changed its tense.

For want of an agent, the verb was inactive.
Which rendered the sentence less than attractive.

For want of attraction, the wording gave way.
For lack of fixation, the thoughts passed away.

And all for the want of a tittle of ink.

Fate

A pebble spent years in the ocean,
Stirred slightly by each tidal motion:
On reaching dry land
It felt a small hand
That skimmed it back into the ocean.

Page 8, *The Art of Perception*
Some works by the Dutch graphic artist Maurits Cornelis
Escher (1898 – 1972) feature impossible-looking objects,
such as a staircase. Bathmophobia, a fear of stairs, is
not the same as acrophobia, a fear of heights.

Page 14, *A Taste of History*
Milkybar is a registered trademark of the Nestlé company.
The Milkybar Kid first appeared in advertisements in 1961.

Page 16, *The Mullets and Bars Forever*
The Washington family coat of arms was a white shield
with three mullets above two horizontal red bars.
A mullet, part of a spur, was shown as a five-pointed
star-shape with a central hole.
A fess (plural: bars) represented a military belt.

Page 25, *When Summer Never Came*
A volcano, Mount Tambora in the Dutch East Indies
(Indonesia), erupted in 1815, causing 1816 to become
known as the year without a summer.

Page 32, *Only a Bird*
The Red List of Threatened Species is produced by the
International Union for Conservation of Nature and their
partners. Skylark numbers have declined dramatically
in Britain.

Page 33, *Like a Leaf in Autumn*
Chalara die-back was first confirmed in Britain in 2012.
This disease of ash trees is caused by a fungus,
Hymenoscyphus fraxineus.

Page 50, *Knowing Your Place*
Hræfn is an Old English word for raven. In the poem,
the young man's characteristics are based on the
appearance and observed behaviour of ravens.
Æsc means ash tree and was also a person's name.

Page 54, *The Hedge Cutter*
Inspired by a late 18th century portrait at
Broughton Castle, Oxfordshire.

Page 56, *Below Stairs*
In 16th century England it was made high treason
for a Roman Catholic priest to enter the country.
Wealthy families built hiding places to shelter priests.

Page 59, *Seasoning*
In Japanese, *haiku* (formerly *hokku*) usually convey a
feeling about nature. They have no title, no rhyme,
and minimal punctuation. They are structured in
sounds (*on*), not syllables.

Page 62, *Blackthorn Winter*
A blackthorn winter is a term for when snow falls in
the spring, from the bush that blossoms at that time.

Page 65, *For Want of a Tittle*
tittle: a dot over the lower-case letters i and j.
dagger: a symbol † used to indicate a footnote.
ellipsis: three dots ... to denote that text is omitted.

Printed in Poland
by Amazon Fulfillment
Poland Sp. z o.o., Wrocław

30798017R00043